LEARN TO SPEAK CAT

summersdale

LEARN TO SPEAK CAT

Copyright © Anthony T. Smith, 2009

The right of Anthony T. Smith to be identified as the author of this work has been asserted in accordance with sections 77 and 78 of the Copyright, Designs and Patents Act 1988.

Summersdale Publishers Ltd
46 West Street
Chichester
West Sussex
PO19 1RP
UK

www.summersdale.com

Printed and bound in China

ISBN: 978-1-84953-003-3

Substantial discounts on bulk quantities of Summersdale books are available to corporations, professional associations and other organisations. For details telephone Summersdale Publishers on (+44-1243-771107), fax (+44-1243-786300) or email (nicky@summersdale.com).

LEARN TO SPEAK CAT

ANTHONY T. SMITH

FEED ME.

I'VE HURT MY FOOT!

I'VE HURT
MY OTHER FOOT!

NOW LOOK WHAT
YOU'VE MADE
ME DO!

ME-OUTH

PUT FOOD IN HERE.

I'M OFF OUT.

THIS IS MY OWL
IMPERSONATION.

I'M GOING OUT FOR
A STROLL.

ME~OUSE

I'VE JUST
EATEN A MOUSE.

FUR BALL, ANYONE?

HSS!

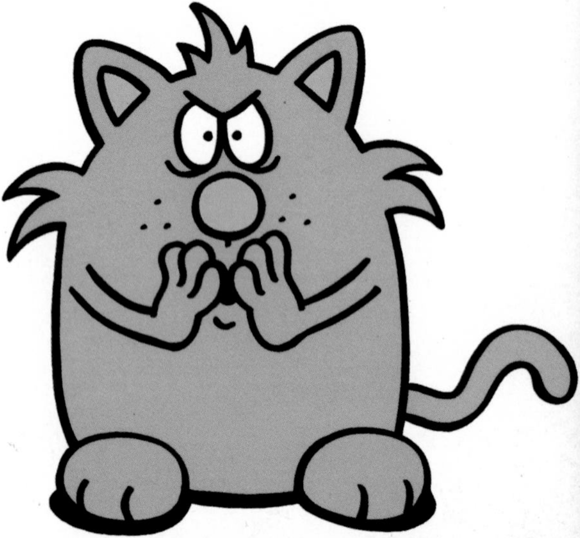

BOO!

REALLY BIG SNAKE!

THERE'S A
POSSIBILITY THAT I'VE
PUNCTURED YOUR LILO.

YOUR SISTER CALLED.

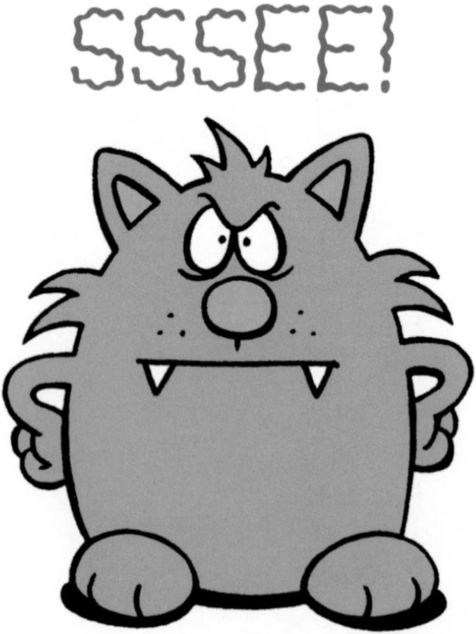
SSSEE!

TOLD YOU!

I'M FEELING POORLY.

LET'S HAVE A ROW.

RI~OW

LET'S GO TO RIO.

DID YOU SEE THE
FORMULA 1
LAST NIGHT?

PURÉE THAT FOR ME.

GO AND BUY ME SOME
CAT FOOD.

EAT MY DUST.

I'VE STILL GOT IT.

HEY, NICE BUM.

POORRR

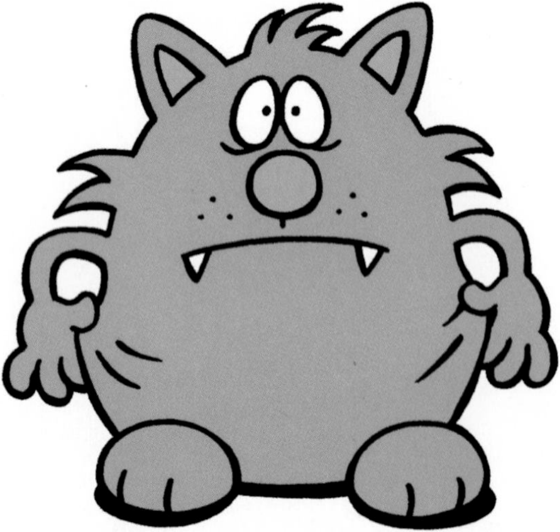

I'M A BIT STRAPPED
FOR CASH.

START POURING.

HEY YOU.

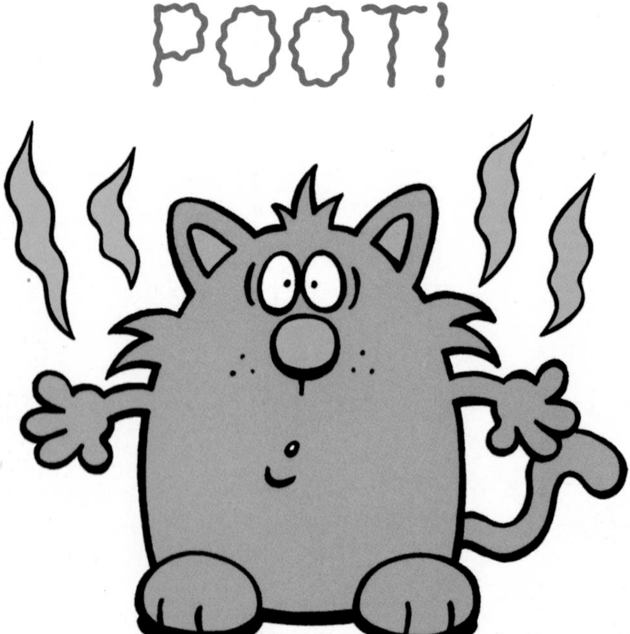
POOT!

OH, DO EXCUSE ME.

MOI?

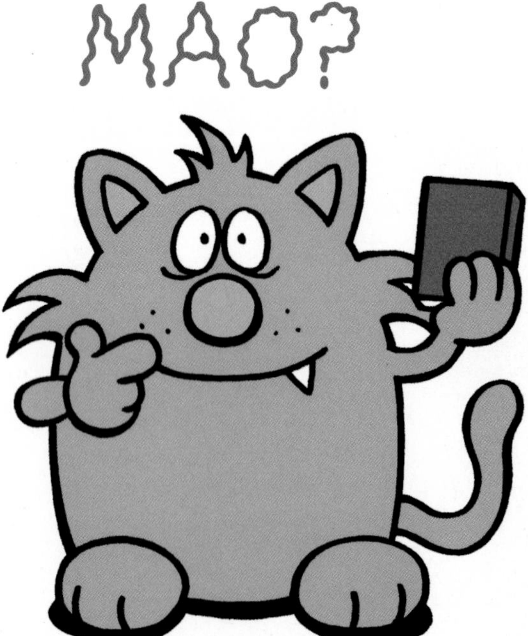
MAO?

HAVE YOU READ
THE WORKS OF THE
LATE CHAIRMAN?

MOW!

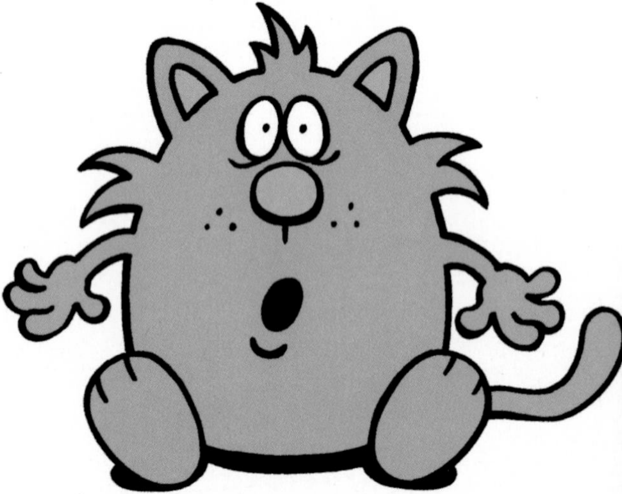

MOU~SEE

LOOK, A MOUSE.

DO YOU SPEAK MAORI?

ME-AM

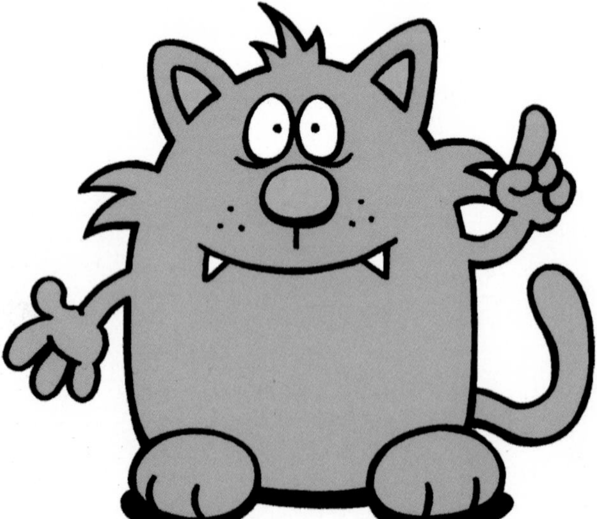

I THINK,
THEREFORE I AM.

NO SMOKING PLEASE.

IT'S JUST US, THEN?

WHAT'S FOR DINNER?

URP

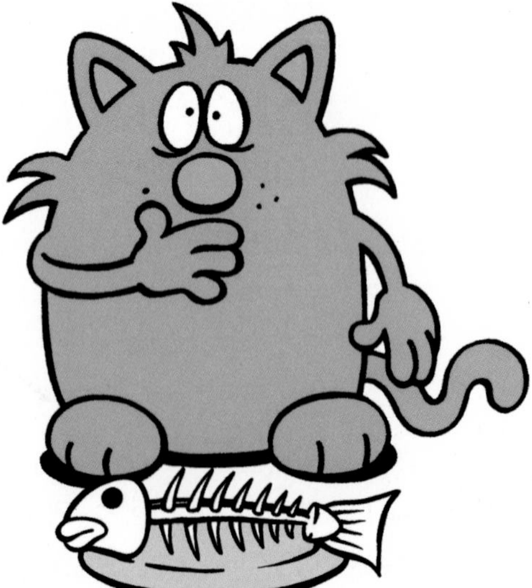

MY COMPLIMENTS
TO THE CHEF.

CAN I HAVE
SOME MORE?

GIVE ME MILK.

I DON'T EAT
THAT DRY STUFF.

BLURG

I SHALL NOT BE
RECOMMENDING THE FOOD
IN THIS ESTABLISHMENT.

I'M GOING TO MAKE
A FUSS NOW.

ME-AH

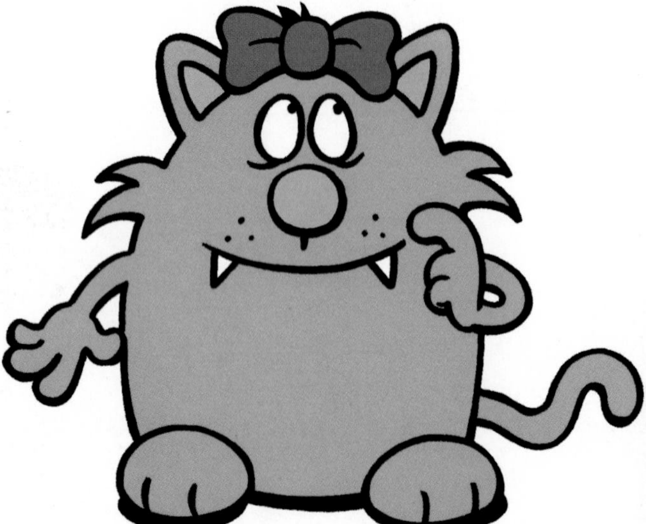

LOVABLE, AREN'T I?

ME-OWF!

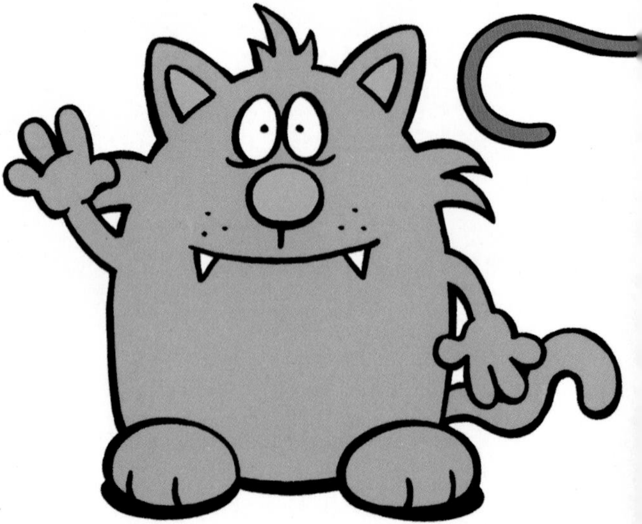

THANK YOU AND GOODNIGHT!

Have you enjoyed this book?
If so, why not write a review
on your favourite website?

Thanks very much for buying
this Summersdale book.

www.summersdale.com